Asia For Kids
People, Places and Cultures
Children Explore The World Books

BABY PROFESSOR

EDUCATION KIDS

ASIA
Fun Facts

Asia is the largest continent on Earth: It covers almost 9% of the globe and just under a third of the total land mass of the planet.

Asia Has the Most Varied Landscape

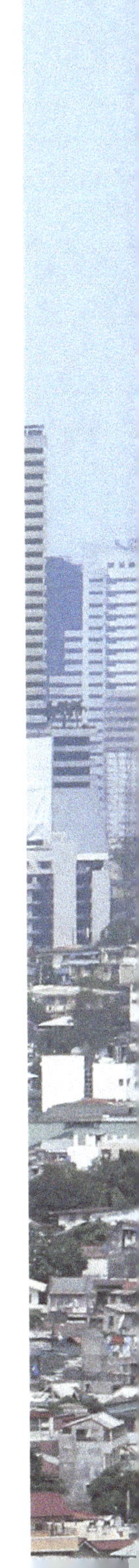

7 of the World's 10 Most Densely Populated Cities are in Asia

Asia's Population Is Larger than the Rest of The World Combined

Asia is Home to 9 of the World's 10 Tallest Buildings

The highest
point on earth,
Mt. Everest,
is in Asia. The
lowest point
on land, the
Dead Sea, is
also in Asia.

Asia is home to many interesting animals including the giant panda, Asian elephant, tiger, Bactrian camel, komodo dragon, and the king cobra.

China Is the World's Third Largest Country yet it Has Only One Time Zone

Over 4,000
Chinese
Children
Are Named
'Olympic
Games'

It's Illegal
to Be Fat
in Japan

Vietnamese New Year Is Everybody's Birthday

The Thai Celebrate New Years with Water Pistols

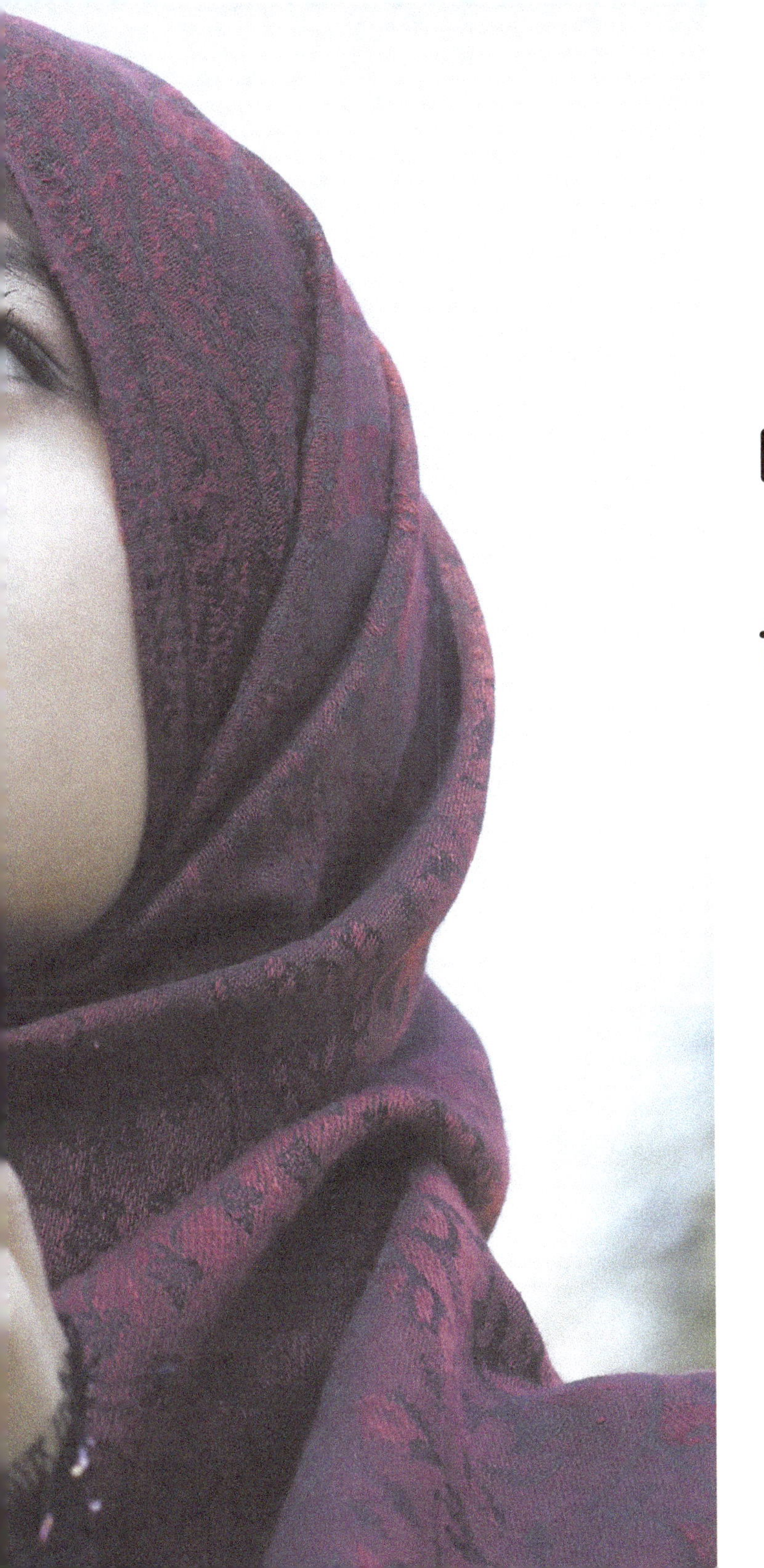

In South Asia live more Muslims than in the whole Middle East, yet Muslims in South Asia is less than 15% of total population.

The World's Largest Shopping Mall Is A Ghost Town

Indians Eat With The Right Hand, Wipe With The Left

Maldives is 99% Muslim country. In Maldives it is illegal for tourists have more than 1 Bible, because they fear that tourists can give it to local people.

Asian business is booming and many of the things you use or wear every day were probably made in Asia, from the gadget you listen to music on, to your socks and the kettle you need to make a cuppa.

Asia's three dominant financial centers are Tokyo, Hong Kong and Singapore.

Visit
BABY PROFESSOR
EDUCATION KIDS
www.BabyProfessorBooks.com
to download Free Baby Professor eBooks
and view our catalog of new and exciting
Children's Books